Time the Unfound Friend©

By Dr. Mark D. White

In this world, all you have to do in life is

decide what to do with the

time given you!

(JRR Tolkien)

Visit www.markwhite.tv for updated contact information.

Printed and Manufactured in the United States

For additional copies of this book and other resources,

Contact Dr. Mark D. White by email: rapha@gmx.us or zdkadar@gmail.com

ISBN-13: 978-1508553588
ISBN-10: 1508553580

DEDICATION

Nothing in life can be balanced without friends and family. Thank God for my friends and family. Priorities are the creators of peace and harmony. Thank you Jesus for all that you have done for me! From old friends to new friends, God put you in my life for seasons and reasons. Thank you for the part you played in shaping my tomorrow!

Kim, Seth, Jordan, Anna, Ricky & Eva, Jeff & Jan, Margie, Betty, Shane & Cristy, Bill & Robin, Tommy, Ray, Melody & Mike, David, Debbie, John & Aimee, Kevin & Karen, David & Clara, Mark, Greg, Barnie, Charles, Robin, Gloria, Guy & Patricia, Dan & Shelby, Dominique & Bridgett, Seraphin & Ines

The sun is setting while night time slips in. The moments are changing as one day comes to an end. As the sun is setting, it still rises as a new day begins. From east to west while the process takes hold without end, Still it is new cycle that is like the blowing of the wind.. But now are my choices playing a role in this lifes cycle that seems without end? Seasons come and seasons go.. But is my harvest totally in the seeds I sow.. Somewhere the grace and mercy of God takes hold of me.. And just like the Sun rises, it's a new day for me.. So destiny, destiny you call me by name.. For God is creating something's new, a life full of change and I'm not sure what to do while the old seems to keep happening inspite of what do and I pursue!

By Mark D. White©

Contents:

Introduction

Time is the very thing that God used to create the universe. There is no mathematics or sound waves or speed of light without the power of time. Time is the element that God releases when He said in Genesis 1:1-6 "In the beginning" and then "Let there be" and there was light and He separated light from darkness. There is no flow of blood or rhythm of a heart beating without the power and influence of time. Blood makes a complete circle in your body every 22 seconds.

The corresponding actions of thought and action in our lives correlates one's response with attitude, feelings and imagination. From music to singing everything is coexistent with the measure of time allowed in one's life. From birth to death the accounting of our lives in birthdays to experience and accomplishments is regulated by time.

I use the analogy of time as a friend to emphasize the power and influence that you can increase in your life if you will become a close friend with time. In making a relationship strong it takes time which will change your life

In this allowing everyone you love to experience the blessings of meeting your BFF best friend forever called Time. The circumference of the moon is the influence to the tides that rises and falls on the shores around this earth. Time is the force, power and greatest influence that rules in every nation, every situation to set in motion all of creation to a place called accountability.

Chapter One

Finding the friend called Time

As you read this, you may find the surprise of a lifetime is in a key element called time. Life without time is like a heart that has no beat, there is no life's blood flowing, music cannot be played without time and the future cannot exist without a past. The very essence called time can be lost or found, wasted or invested but never returned.

Time is the very priceless element that can't be taken from you without you being distracted or negligent. Time is the very element that can just disappear or seems to be quickly taken from us by some unseen force. **Time is the most valuable priceless possession an individual can have.**

The consistent application of one's desire and disciplined works often brings fulfillment as time the Unfound Friend comes and goes in our lives. Cambridge University scientists have found that the circadian clock is in red blood cells with a 24 hour rhythm.

Time is made up of 60 seconds in a minute, with 60 minutes in an hour, with 24 hours in a day, with 168 hours in a week with time in a continuum throughout your life. Your self-discipline multiplies results with the help of an Unfound Friend called Time. This relationship helps in yielding a plan which

Time is the hidden treasure that if lost, its hard to find again.

is more than an idea, but a commitment in oversight. This works a vision or a dream into the application of your time where success can happen with consistency

With any relationship, your Unfound Friend called Time, is cherished and appreciated in your thoughts, mindset, and desires as one's age becomes a factor in times spent and time remembered. Even your very best friends can get on your nerves because of not having enough time or even having to wait longer than desired, because the clock of patience has stopped.

Everyone on this earth has the same amount of time. From continent to continent, the management of 168 hours varies as each culture has influenced how Time is applied. From male to female your schedule of when you get out of bed and when you go to bed has been created by the influence of others.

A friend of mine years ago named Buck Thomas, told me that there are two systems in this world, the one that exist and the one you create. The only thing is, the system that exists will not mke room for you to create a new system or a way of doing things. You will have to build on principle; not necessity. Time is often too short to debate with others about the desires of your heart.

This is so true, the more I travel the world telling people of the Love of Jesus. I have seen culture, personalities and even gender expect you to comply and change to what they are used to. **That is why you must settle the issue; you cannot discipline your time if you cannot discipline your mind.** In this world, all you have to do in life is decide what to do with the time given you!

You can almost measure time by your very own needs, wants and desires, these issues challenge the power of patience. Even the power of confusion or even not knowing what to do is really based on fear. The excuses of "what ifs" or "yea buts" feed confusion. The power of commitment is a choice before it reaches the heart and that is where passion begins. Confusion is the result of being afraid to make a decision, with the excuse of not knowing what to do and **"If you live off of excuses, you could die because of the reasons."**

Time is created in the spirit realm, though some think there is no time in the spirit realm. The creator of Heaven and earth also created time, He set in motion the rising and setting of the sun, which really is the rotation of the earth. The cycle of the tides of the oceans are regulated by the distance and rotation of the moon.

Having a vision, a dream with a plan can cause a passionate desire to be created, which causes the creation of a new tomorrow. Doing something different does not always change tomorrow, but changing the way you see and hear can cause change. Like seeing with your ears and hearing with your eyes, this can bring change. My thoughts affect what I say and who or what I spend time with, this causes the results of my life.

Time with its lack of management can be lost, mishandled or even seems to be shortened to the point of despair in some lives. Time can't be bought, borrowed, or stolen. In everything in life, what you take for granted can be taken from you before you realize it. Time is such a powerful force that in the book of Acts chapter one verse seven tells us, "Jehovah God who created the whole universe reserves the right to control time and its seasons." What you do when the Unfound Friend called Time affects your decisions and seasons which determine the outcome of long lasting results and relationships.

Notes_____

_____

_____

_____

_____

_____

_____

_____

_____

Chapter Two
TIME and LIGHT

Time and light are synonymous, and you can't have one without the other. Even in the darkest dark, only with light can anything be measured. Even in the existence of the atom the very center of the atom is called a quark. The quark is the sound that creates the light of the atom and its colors. Remembering the old story which if a tree falls in the woods and nothing or no one hears it, it makes no sound. There is sound everywhere even if there are not ears to hear.

Even the sound of a quark in the core of an atom is life continuing to grow. The speed of light and the breaking of the sound barrier are entwined together. It takes the speed of sound to travel 1100 feet per second. For those of you in the metric system it takes about 366 meters per second for sound to go into another dimension, which is about one mile covered within five seconds. For when you have gone faster than sound you still have light there for you to calculate the comparison at that place. I remember when I took Karate; the speed of a response was just as effective as the power. That is just part of the initial importance of the power and influence of Time which is the friend of the Atom.

The spirit realm is the only place when the speed of light is matched and applied beyond the speed of sound. That is why creation is more than evolution it is desires set in motion with the words of God simply stated "Let it be" in book of Genesis. God hears your thoughts before you release your words that are always in a time continuum. Even the sequenced rhythm of your heart, with every beat is the sound of life.

It is when time stops that your spirit leaves your body; as you exit one dimension to enter another.

Because of the blood of Jesus we can live in two worlds as we are repeating and creating the sounds of Heaven. With your words you can create a different tomorrow or recreate your past. Words are eternal and darkness has no end, for you cannot measure darkness without sound and you need light to measure sound. Light is there before you see it, God knows what you have need of before you ask (Matthew 6:8).

With words and time music is created and established as a powerful force that can soote the soul while minimizing stress or create a physical response

Notes_____

_____

_____

to the time in the music of keeping the beat. Jesus Christ, being the light of the world has everything to do with creation; healings, miracles, and eternity even though He is like a Phantom Limb relating to what is really not seen but is still there.

The spirit realm is more real to some individuals because they can feel, can sense, and even know what is there that others cannot. For in darkness there is no knowledge of what is coming or whatever can be controlled or prevented, unless there is sound and light. The power of light or insight gives everyone the opportunity of authority in controlling time by regulation and delegation. Really it seems if anyone would yield and invest the power of time in a relationship with Jehovah God, a new creation takes place; as stated in Joshua 1:8 and II Corinthians 5:17

Your investment of time can give you right relationships; secure environments, economic returns that are short-term and long-term rewards. But all investments of time have to do with a plan, purpose and a desired accomplishment or pursuilt.

Proverbs 29:18 tells us of a people without a goal, a vision, a desired accomplishment; are a people without results, progressive accomplishments and no guidelines or perimeters to keep focus for lasting results. The book of Proverbs also describes a fool as one that is unconscious of responsibility ... Proverbs 17:24 "The discerning person looks to wisdom, but the eyes of a fool to the ends of the earth."

Notes_____

_____

_____

We can all give up on life and treat the future as though it's over or you can be an optimist and seize the day by choosing a moment to change the future and remember that Jesus paid for your past and future, but you pay for your moment! Finding time, you know I am talking about your Unfound Friend, the all elusive situation and structured pursuits of the melting pot of multi-tasking individuals.

Even in the structure of our thinking and processing, the shadow of one's mind is based upon memories that are only remembered by the light or insight of something else called memories of association.

Notes

_____

_____

_____

In the world of getting older this does not mean one is getting wiser, even though we all should try, because knowl-edge is very profitable. It is amazing as we age as adults, our children or grandchildren bring to light memories that we vaguely remember until someone walks in our shadow following our footsteps.

But, no one on this planet earth can wake up every morning, after every morning and still believe the lie of life is over, it's over and there is no use to live. Life will go on just like time is a continuum, with or without you.

The space created between light and time has created the opportunity to see into the spirit realm and take in knowledge that only you can understand. Maybe your thoughts are pessimistic or negative and you think that you might as well give up.

Notes_____

_____

If these are your thoughts, you can still get up to pursue some kind of act of faith toward changing your moment which can affect the rest of your life. The very fact that you eat, put clothes on, is tellingme there is hope.

Even the shame or past experiences that we try to cover up can feed our hope, just the feeling of never wanting to go through that type of situation again can motivate you to captivate your moment for investment of change. With the power of basic scriptures knowledge onecan cover his or her past, while creating hope for a better future. It is like the Chinese proverb "How do you walk a thousand miles? Just one step at a time!

Notes_____

_____

_____

Jesus Christ said in John 3:19-20 that those that want change will take action to expose their weakness and fallacies. Those that want to hang on to hiding under darkness or keeping things under wrap, stay away from the light. The only issue is, Jesus is the light. In John 8:12 Jesus said, "I am the light of the world. Whoever follows me will never walk in darkness but will have the light of life. This means there will come wisdom and understanding by the Holy Spirit (John 14:26).

There is an element of safety with walking in the light versus walking in darkness. I have bee in a coal mine about half a mile under the earth; in turning out the light,

Notes_____

_____

_____

_____

_____

no one can see their hand in front of their face. In darkness nothing can be measured without sound and sound requires light for results. Words create light and light gives insight while insight creates opportunity while your Unfound Friend called Time changes the moment!

Knowing some facts about time can easily be challenged with a moment of surprise taking place in your life. Whether it's good or bad circumstances these can seem to take over the power of committed or delegated time. From earthquakes to severe weather or health issues which can threaten one's life. To making time a priority for your children, seeing they are only little boys or little girls once in life.

Notes_____

_____

Children get lost in time and we as parents, if we can find the Unfound Friend called Time, we can change the moments and create cherished memories.

This amplifies even more reason why one needs to be led by the spirit of God which dwells within the born again believers. Our God Jehovah is the all-knowing God, omnipotent, omniscient, omnipresent mighty God. Because of His Son Jesus, His Holy Spirit can give you understanding in many different ways concerning your future.

The process of working with the power of the Holy Spirit can seem to stretch time or condense it. But, knowing this and going beyond the natural in the spirit realm can place you where there is no time. Again I say that knowing this & going beyond the natural will in the spirit realm place you where there is no time. In the books Mark 4:22 and Matthew 10:26, both state almost the same thing, "for there is nothing hidden, except that that it be exposed; nor is anything secret, except to come to light". 23 "let anyone with ears to hear listen!" 24 "And he said to them, Pay attention to what you hear; the measure you give will be the measure you get, and still more will be given you". 25 "For to those who have, more will be given; and from those who have nothing, even what they have will be taken away. " Excuses are a standard of those which have no hope or faith of a future or destiny.

The priceless item called time which is bought and sold in the market place, can become the item that cannot be found or managed. Time is the Unfound Friend, for when you can find it; it excels your abilities to accomplishments or success. When you can't time, it seems to amplify problems in our lives. When you recognize time as your best friend you always want to keep in close contact with him/her and know where he/she is at; at all times.

If you are blaming the devil for stealing, your life, your money, your relationships, your health, your future, I ask, is it just the devil or is there the need of increased management and stewardship of your time and your mind? I know the Devil is here to steal, kill, and destroy (John 10:10). The book of James 3 tells us where confusion and strife are, it is giving every opportunity for the devil. But is it possible we have been "asleep at the wheel" and we

Notes_____

_____   _____

_____

have taken time for-granted, while taking our lives, relationships, possessions, even our health for granted also. **Reality is, what you take for-granted can be taken from you.**

Our life reflects our choices, even though to some of us it seems we have done everything to stand and resist the Devil. But I ask, are we doing everything and still doing nothing to stand according to God's Word? "For if you live by excuses you will die because of the reasons." Standing is not a one-time experience. Just like being filled with the Holy Spirit, is not a one-time experience, but a lifetime pursuit. It is like breathing, when you pause and take a break from breathing, you may not wake up.

*Notes*_____

_____

The cost of your tomorrow is invested in your today. Just like the price of having good health has a price of eating right and exercise while taking good care of this body,which is the temple of God on this earth. As stated in Galatians 6:7 "what you sow is what you reap." So, in being a doer of the word and not just a hearer only is an active lifestyle of choice pursuits (James 1:22).

Again the book of Acts in chapter one with verse seven tells us that the Father reserves the right to control time and seasons. The element of time invested is what controls your mind. This affects your attitude, while your emotions come from your mind. "The fruit of your lips comes from the seed of your thoughts." For, as a one thinks, so are they.

Notes_____

_____

My imagination is just part of my limitation, my meditation is just a small part of my activation for my manifestation is my conformation of what I can disciple in this life is what I have disciplined in my mind and thoughts. In the book of 2nd Corinthians chapter ten with verse five, we are instructed to cast down the very thoughts which disagree with God and His knowledge of your future.

Your life can be the repetition of your past, someone's influence, or be the creation of pursuits that bring change. You can recreate your past with negligence or you can create you a new future with disciplined committed investment. **Lining up your choices with the word of God, causes everything to start flowing toward peace, love and joy with the Holy Spirit (Romans 14:17).**

Start your day spending time as an investment. Spend time reading your Bible, praying, meditating and setting a course of accomplishments for the day. Your vision or desires create your victories. When there are no desires, nor vision, there are no victories in our lives.

We seem hopeless without our blessed hope (Titus 2:13) Jesus Christ as the greatest influence of our life. It is like this same concept I live by, "what you feed grows and what you starve dies." Seek to know and be known by Jesus and his Angels. Demons fear what Angels respect and protect. Your time invested relationship with the Holy Spirit causes your whole life to change the way Heaven wants one's life to live. Investing in your eternity is like investing in your next

Notes_____

breath; you will reap the rewards of this investment forever (Galatians 6:8). Remember a seed is more than a thought; it can change your life forever. **Time is short and eternity is at hand, if you were judged right now where would you stand?**

Eternity is like infinity, the beginning is only a step toward a never ending story. Time is so priceless that the only ones that can hardly wait are what we call counting down to the anticipated moment. The other side is counting the time that has gained contradiction of someone who thought they could put a time limit on new beginnings. Really you are never prepared to live till you are totally prepared to die. With that issue settled life can be a party, an adventure or a bucket list of things to accomplish in a period of time.

Notes_____

Notes_____

_____

_____

_____

_____

_____

_____

_____

Chapter 3
The Power Of Patience

Watching someone who says they are in control while they begin to lose control emotionally is a troubling moment. Life's challenges at times can be overwhelming and because a person's has self-discipline issues. At times their lack of patience can really remove emotional stability while trust turns to judgment with condemnation; this is because of a issue called self-control. **Patience is not a duration of time, but a frame of your mind.** It literary is the power to stop the control that circumstances, situations and pressure from other people tend to create.

Notes_____

_____

In the Gospel of Luke in chapter 21:19 an awesome statement is hid between the lines. "In your patience possess ye your souls." In one way of thinking, patience is more of an attitude, it's a mindset. **Patience comes with peace; it works hand in hand while time seems evasive.** You cannot have patience if you lose your temper or get frustrated when time is not according to your will.

For when you lose peace you begin to lose your self-control called patience. You cannot opperate in faith without patience (Hebrews 6:12) and you cannot maintain faith without peace. Time defined is the very foundation and standard for the definition of patience.

Notes_____

_____

The synonyms for patience are forbearance, long-suffering, sufferance, tolerance and all of these are part of a period in which time is the factor in question. Your attitude is the display of humility because you have peace, self-control, patience and the adjustable moment of power called attitude. It is impossible to keep a level head and lead by example when one is easily impatient or emotionally responsive.

The atmosphere can be changed in a room because of one person's attitude going bad because they had no patience. In every area of relationships; the price of love is time. Once you have experienced love, you are affected in some way the rest of your life to the influence of a friend called time.

Notes_____

_____

_____

Jesus is called the Prince of Peace, to really carry such a title you have to be full of patience, love, forgiveness and a strong amount of temperance also known as tolerance of others. In 2 Peter 3:8-9 reads: "But do not forget this one thing:

With the Lord a day is like a thousand years, and a thousand years are like a day. The Lord Jesus is not slow in keeping his promise, as some understand slowness. He is patient with you, not wanting anyone to perish, but everyone to come to repentance." The book of Isaiah 40:31 tells us of waiting on the Lord (Jehovah God). Which causes us to have renewed strength and to mount up with wings as Eagles in comparison.

Notes_____

_____

We will run and not get tired or walk and not give up; that means we have patience. These comparisons give us an idea of the reach beyond our understanding to go beyond the limits that seem to be imposed on us. In the spirit realm there is no element as what we called time.

Even the speed of light exceeds the speed of sound. Throughout the years the sought out knowledge of a time machine was such a great dream. To change the past from being repetitive means to change the future application of increased knowledge.

This means learning must begin without an ending. This is so true, if you do not want to repeat the past, invest some of your mind, your will and your emotions on a friend called time. This investment is of continuous educational expansion in one's life, changes everything. I find that when it comes to knowing the will of God,

I ask myself these questions. Can I talk myself into it? If so, I can talk myself out of it, but when it's God's will for your life, you do not have to talk yourself into it or neither can you talk yourself out of it. A friend called time could be invested as a continuous educational expansion in one's life.

In the book of Matthew chapter 6 with verses 19 through 23 the scripture tells us the diverse management of short term and long term investments. (19) "Lay not up for yourselves treasures upon earth, where moth and rust doth corrupt, and where thieves break through and steal: (20) "But lay up for yourselves treasures in heaven, where neither moth nor rust doth

Notes_____

_____

_____

corrupt and where thieves do not break through nor steal: (21) "For where your treasure is, there will your heart be also. (22) "The light of the body is the eye: if therefore thine eye be single, thy whole body shall be full of light." (23) "But if thine eye be evil, thy whole body shall be full of darkness. If therefore the light that is in thee be darkness, how great is that darkness!

We had talked earlier about darkness and about measuring in darkness requires sound and sound and light are the same. It is in the Atom the composite breakdown of this going nuclear which is really a Quark which is a re-creative sound made in the research of an atom. In the wisdom of the aged, our schedule, our programs and our accomplishments are time based issues

Notes_____

_____

which when the illusive; but so much needed can be found, it's about our Unfound Friend Called Time.

Time has created a new world of knowledge based on the age of all creation, which is solidified by time against time. The Bible is your greatest asset for measuring and balancing your life, the in's and out's, the up's and even the down's can be balanced, establishing a rule of thumb for guarding and accomplishing the greatest results in your life. Proverbs 3:21in the (N IV©1984) puts this in perspective, "My son, preserve sound judgment and discernment, do not let them out of your sight".

Notes_____

_____

_____

_____

Then in Proverbs chapter 4:20 "My son, attend to my words; incline thine ear unto my sayings. Let them not depart from thine eyes; keep them in the midst of thine heart. For they are life unto those that find them, and health to all their flesh. Keep thy heart with all diligence; for out of it are the issues of life. Put away from thee a forward mouth, and perverse lips put far from thee. Let thine eyes look right on, and let thine eyelids look straight before thee. Ponder the path of thy feet, and let all thy ways be established. Turn not to the right hand nor to the left: remove thy foot from evil. It takes working with time to do all of this.

The road map in life should not only get you where you want to be on this earth, but should take you into paradise also known as Heaven after your death. Really to put time as a relational issue, the measure that you seek God will be the measure of people seeking you.

The amount of time you spend in His presence causes the power of prayer to change lives quickly. Trusting God is different than trusting people; people make mistakes God never does, so if you can trust God with your eternity, why can't you trust Him with your today. It is just as simple as stated in Proverbs 8:14"Advice and priceless wisdom are mine. I, Understanding, have strength" (GWD® Translation©1995). Knowledge is Power! Time as I have stated is your Unfound Friend, when your life is diligent and not slothful you will understand this one statement. There seems never to be enough time in a day, but when you spend time building a relational time table or a system.

Notes_____

_____

The structure of time is priceless for you. You will find the Unfound Friend called Time and the relationship will be most profitable and influential in your life.

Never Procrastinate, never yield to Procrastination. Never!

Regulating, delegating and mandating causes the commodity called time to be one of your greatest investments and greatest friends. One of my professors in college gave me a principle that I will never forget. He called them the four D's of priority, you do what you can do, delegate what you can and delay what you have to and then delete the rest. The law of Sowing and Reaping has been established from the beginning of time, even in Galatian's chapter 6 verse 7, "God is not taken lightly or irrelevant, for what you the individual sow (plant in life) you will reap in this life."

Never procrastinate, never yield to Procrastination. Never! If your choice in seeking God was as the beat of your heart or your next breath. Could you, should you Procrastinate. Eternity is only a breath away! Praying for you that read this! That God will put in your heart a hunger for His Word, a hunger for His Presence, a hunger for His Ways.

Chapter 4

Is Time on your Hands or Blood?

Once upon a time is a great beginning for fantasy, but what I am telling you really happened to me. Years ago, I was walking the perimeter of the church I pastored and was praying. As I was praying I looked up on the thresh hold of the doors to the entrance to the auditorium and had an open vision. I saw two hands, one was filled with dripping blood and the other was holding an hour glass.

As I was so focused on what I was seeing, I heard a voice speak to me and said, "Is time on your hands or blood?" Then immediately a scroll with the scripture of Ezekiel 3:17-21 came to me as I fell on my knees overwhelmed with this vision and God encounter. The very context of the scripture strongly addresses the responsibility of what is called a watchman. The watchman is one who sounds off an alarm for warning and announcing what the enemy is doing. In second Thessalonians chapter two the issue of the mystery of iniquity is brought to discussion and the end results of deception. Judas was one of those that thought he knew more than God.

There are a lot of good people out there with good hearts but stupid heads. God requires that we yield our control of knowledge to Him, as so stated in Proverbs 3:5 tells us to "Trust in the Lord with all our hearts and lean not to our understanding." In the book of Romans 8:14 the Apostle Paul states that those who are led by the Spirit are the Sons of God or mature ones or responsible individuals, dependable, faithful ones. There is a thing called iniquity which is lawlessness or also known as lasciviousness, which can be defined as not being disciplined toward the truth. Remember, if you cannot control your mind, you will never control your time. It's like scuba diving and the passing of your diving certification is the proof there is a discipline in your response.

Which means circumstances do not make you lose control of how you respond. Time is the most important factor while you are underwater and in need of some oxygen. But how you use wisdom and application determines panic or self-control as patience gets you to the flow of air to breath. Your own emotional response can be your Judas that sells out your moment and controls your future. In II Corinthians 10:3-5 you are at war so control your thoughts like God.

It is easy to drown in your circumstances if you do not use time wisely. With the power of agreement with your Unfound Friend called Time. You can seek, find and apply knowledge where you are not the servant of circumstances. Your own words can connect hope to cope and cope to endurance and endurance to accomplishments. **Remember if Satan can manipulate your emotions, He can manipulate your lifestyle.**

James 1:2 tells us to "Consider all of things joyfully during the test of your faithfulness and knowing patience is the strongest element to cause peace with expectancy which is needed to fulfill the desired faith's manifestation. Again, Patience is not a duration of time, but the frame of your mind, patience is the strength of a good leader. Impatient people make poor leaders and patient leaders have committed followers.

As stated in Hebrews 6:12 that with faith and patience we obtain the promise. So do you have time on your hands or blood?

Your responsibility with your family or the lives of others is based on how your manage time. From being a Doctor, Nurse, Policeman, to a Senator or just management to a team member, you are responsible for other people in one form or another. Even in driving a car or flying a plane you have a reaction based on your actions. If you can control and know time, you can change tomorrow.

Notes_____

_____

_____

_____

Chapter 5

Opportunity Robbed and Protection Missed

I have never been one which overlooks the symbolic nature of a thief. These types of people take what is not theirs without any consideration of the owner. The statement that time is ticking and ticking away is so untrue, time happens without a sound. As the sun rises and the moon sets the cycle of life continues with or without our acknowledgement.

In this chapter we deal with stealing from God the honor we should give Him, but that we give to others and ourselves. God created time and I understand that love believes the best, but love is not stupid or blind and stupid is as stupid does! Our lives are to represent the creator of the universe and not the destroyer of hope.

Usually I have no problem forgiving someone, but trust has to be re-earned from an old friend as much as a new one when wrong has been perpetrated. Even God has standards of evaluating commitment to covenant. For if you live off excuses, you can die because of the reasons! For the spirit realm is not set up for the flesh to have a say so in eternaty issues.

Trusting God is trusting the unseen, at times the unheard and even unfelt. The power of a magnet is an unseen force. Watching the trees move with the wind is an unseen force, Gravity is an unseen force and all that we mentioned is created by the one true God Jehovah and in all that is mentioned what you cannot see is moving what you see.

Giving honor to whom honor is due is stated in Romans 13 and Rev. 4:11. Giving honor is a time oriented application, attitude, actions, atmosphere all contribute to celebration of the one person to honor is bestowed.

In Psalms 105 verse 19 "Until the time came to fulfill his dreams, the LORD tested Joseph's character" (New Living Translation©2007). Being in prison is bad and very challenging to one's commitment and integrity as the circumstances can be overwhelming. But also being in prison in your mind and being free physically is heart breaking.

Too many people are living a life of limits based on past experiences and not living a dream based on the understanding of God's word for their lives.

Notes_____

_____

_____

Until your Unfound Friend called Time has with your invested seeking of the knowledge of the Lord. Time cannot be replenished and restored from what the devil has stolen from you. What are your character traits? Are you diligent, committed or one that lives off of excuses and blames others?

Back in 1978, I heard this statement, **"Life is what you make it; you choose that yourself"** is a quote that changed my life. **As William Shakespeare says, "to thy own self be true."** Joseph's life changed within hours because of his heartfelt commitment to the word of the Lord. From rags to riches happened within hours, just based on know-ledge that someone remembered about Joseph from being in prison with him. As the situation played out, all those family and friends Joseph knew changed their lives, based on the changes in his. God is so Good!

Chapter 6

Attitude Investments

In the book of Malachi chapter 3 verse 14 the text and content of thescriptures has been misunderstood and misapplied. "Ye have said, It is vain to serve God: and what profit is it that we have kept his ordinance, and that we have walked mournfully before the LORD of hosts" (Geneva Study Bible)? There are principles which are categorically not in writing, but are matters of the heart throughout all of humanity.

No matter what the culture or location in this world, we find ourselves being just like everybody else or we make a decision to stand on principals of the heart which at times does not find agreement with others or even the unseen mandates expected by others.

Serving God is a matter of the heart, not one of what we can always see or feel, touch, taste and even smell. "The promises of God are yes and amen" (II Corinthians 1:20). Malachi chapter 3 verse 6 states that Gods integrity is the same for all generations. But then He asks this question inverse 8, "Will a man rob God? That is a wild statement. How do you rob from someone who has everything, knows everything, and is all powerful?

The question is not what we take from Him, but what we do not give Him, and could that be Honor, which is priceless in building relationships? The issue is not about money, yes I said not about money. But this content of text could be more about

Notes_____

_____

_____

what money represents than what money can do. Money comes from the old friend that we can never find, you know the unfound friend. For in your lifespan we receive compensation for the knowledge we have, the skill we developed and the time we have invested. Just to simplify it, your skill, your will, your time your mind all of these bring and should bring compensation to you during your lifetimeon this planet earth.

If you have a company or you work for a company or even self-employed. You barter or trade your time, your mind, your will and your skill for a compensation that helps secure your lifestyle as you desire it or allow it.The jealous God we serve is just and desires a return on what He freely gives and what He should freely receive back for Him a harvest from our lives.

Notes_____

_____

Jesus gave His life for us that we might give our lives to Him, this is what is called reciprocity, meaning a mutual exchange. He that knew no sin became sin that we might be made the righteousness of God (II Corinthians 5:21), and he that was rich became poor that we might be made rich (II Corinthians 8:9). He paid the price for our redemption from the power of sin and the powers of darkness (Psalms 107:2) (Galatians 3:13,14).

Because of Jesus we have been redeemed from all curses, except for the ones we cause ourselves. We have been redeemed from sin, sickness, poverty and death, because of the blood of Jesus. That is why Galatians 6:7 tells us that God is not taken lightly. God has made a way of escape from life and its troubles (I Corinthians 10:13). But what you do with one of the best friends you could find helps develop and establish success or failure.

That friend is only found when you search and his/her name is Time. Finding time with God is a new tomorrow.   We the people of God have robbed God from being to us who He is; He is our redeemer, our ever present help in the time of trouble. Again I say the church has robbed God from being who He really is, by reliving the law and not being part of the greatest relationship of Grace in the universe.

Honor is such a brief description and a minimal expression of what really should be happening around the world. To give attention to the one that gave so much to humanity as a free gift. We in giving Jesus our time is the beginning of changing the world.

Notes_____

_____

_____

Relationship opens the door for you to become who He is and what He wants to be in your life in this world. John 14:12 tells us the same works He did we can do, then in I John 4:7 it says we can love like Him, I John 4:17 tells us that "As He is, so are we". Then Philippians says that we can do anything though Christ that gives us abilities not known to man. Even as stated in I Peter 2:9 We are called out of darkness to display, to give living proof that we are God's chosen people. He even says He has given us power and authority in the use of His name, Jesus!

The plan of God has no excuse, because the results are set in motion and abilities are without measure if we would allow His Grace to take hold of us. Even in Lamentations 3:22 He speaks of His Mercies are new every morning. Malachi 3:8 says we have robbed God in tithes and offerings which are the foundation of sowing and reaping, the beginning and fulfillment of time. Robbing from God goes beyond money, but starts with time.

We have robbed Him (God) from being who He is to us. Those that cannot tithe because of their lack of trust that God honors His word, it's really character assassination by accusing God of not being faithful to keep His word. There is never a strong relationship without the investment of time. As I have said before, if you can trust God with your eternity, why can't you trust Him with your today?

The unfound friend would point you in the direction of where and when God will fulfill His promises. But it is up to you to seek that you might find and ask that it might be given to you and knock and keep knocking till the doors of opportunity open. As you exchange or barter your skill, your will, your mind and your time for money in this world. God so loved you that He gave and has not stopped giving to you.

All that God wants is a relationship of sowing and reaping. He has giving so much to you that all he wants is the opportunity to be to you who He is. A relationship is not a need oriented issue but of things in common place. Abraham was called the friend of God; Enoch pleased God so much that God took him to heaven without Enoch 's death, Enoch was just no more.

God being a jealous God means he wants a little return on what He has given you. Time is as priceless as a rare diamond. You give time to your work and your work gives you compensation. God wants you to give Him time also and what time represents to the world based on what you bartered. **God wants to be to you who He is!**

He wants to be your healer, your provider, your peace, and the cause of all your joy. As stated in Galatians 6:7, God is not taken lightly or indifferently. He wants to cause a harvest of returns of blessings to you, but what you sow is what you reap. In Malachi 3 He is just telling you that you are robbing from Him the opportunity of being to you who He is.

He is a loving Father, our redeemer but He wants to open the windows of Heaven and pour out upon you who He is as blessings. He wants to be your Jehovah Jirah. . Which means He wants to provide for you all that you need in this life as He will in the life to come. Which means He wants to provide for you all that you need in this life as He will in the life to come. He wants to be your Jehovah Rapha which is the Lord that Heals you.

This open window that should be upon every believer's life is an open portal that causes prayers to be answered and angels to minister to the heirs of salvation, which is you. Because of what God is offering, the believer should live under an Open Heaven and an Open Heaven should live through them. Like the old Hymnal goes, "He's all I need, He's all I need, Jesus is all I need." The issue of tithing is not about money, but what money represents.

The friend of God is time and time wants to be your friend. But you have to find time and when you find your unfound friend called time. You will find a relationship that does not have a problem giving to God money, because time is more valuable than money. Money can be replaced, but time lost is never regained or replaced unless God does it for you.

Yes we serve a miracle working God. By building a relationship based on time with Him, you are building a relationship of trust. This alone is what God wants, where you have faith in His word, you believe in His promises and your stand in agreement with God's Word (the Bible) that He cannot lie. The meaning of tithing is giving God ten percent of what the world gives you for your time, your mind, your will and you skill.

So that He can be to you all that He is because you honor Him enough to be a doer of His word and not just a person that listens, He will be everything to you, for He is the El Shaddai, the God that is more than enough.The seven redemptive names of God and the names that is who Jesus is, are descriptions of character and integrity. Along with the 35 descriptive names of Jesus the level of integrity is high to live up to. A name is a depiction of a person's history & integrity.

That is why honoring God with your first fruits or your tithe is not a law but a door opener of what you sow is what you reap. Honor God and He will honor you! Psalms 26:8 tells us that in God's presence is where we will receive honor from Him. Talk about your name being important, the seven redemptive names of God depict His character and responsibility of being who He is.

1. His name Jehovah Jirah means the Lord that sees and provides.
2. His name Jehovah Rapha means the Lord that healeth thee.
3. The name Jehovah Nisse means the Lord our Banner the declarer of who we are in Him.
4. The name of Jehovah M'Kaddesh means the Lord that sanctifies you.
5. His name Jehovah Shalom means the Lord our Peace.
6. His name Jehovah Tsidkenu means the Lord is our Righteousness.
7. Then His name is Jehovah Rohi which means the Lord our Shepherd.

Knowing who He is; is in knowing His names andwhat He can do and willingly will do as you give Him time and honor, so will He honor you with His presence as the one you need Him to be. Remember that our God changeth not. He is the same yesterday and forever.

Here is the list of the redemptive names of Jesus as well. Even as the history of your integrity is in the identity of your name, so is the name of Jesus as the name that can not lie. Time the Unfound Friend knows all about Jesus, because of the time that Jesus spent seeking God all night long and only doing what He heard and saw God say and do.

And His name shall be called Jesus; Prince of Peace; Mighty God; Wonderful Counselor; Holy One; Lamb of God; Prince of Life; Lord God Almighty; Lion of the Tribe of Judah; Root of David; Word of Life; Author and Finisher of Our Faith; Advocate; The Way; Dayspring; Lord of All; I Am; Son of God; Shepherd and Bishop of Souls; Messiah; The Truth; Saviour;

Chief Cornerstone; King of Kings; Righteous Judge; Light of the World; Head of the Church; Morning Star; Sun of Righteousness; Lord Jesus Christ; Chief Shepherd; Resurrection and Life; Horn of Salvation; Governor and The Alpha and Omega.

With all the description of responsibility of who Jesus is, truly He has a name that is above every name. A name under Heaven that is the only name whereby anyone can be saved (Philippians 2:9-11). Learning the power of the name of Jesus is like going to law school. For He has given us the power of attorney with the use of His name. Only a person that desires to find their unfound friend can take in the knowledge that can change the world. An attitude is what is reflecting what is expected. Thereby affecting everything in your life at that moment.

Chapter 7

What You See is What You Get!

Time management is the only application that can take your life from couch potato to slim trim, lean mean, fighting machine. This is the principle of accomplishments and the difference of procrastination. When time is your best friend and you spend time planning and building a dream and vision of the future. You will see that time will wake you up; time will remind you to go to bed and get some rest; time will remind you of appointments and goals.

Time will remind you of relationships, responsibilities and commitments. Time can be your best friend from the beginning of the day to the end of the week. The only hindrance to a relationship with time is distractions, indifference, excuses, depression, and loss of passion with lack of relational love for the Word of God. Jesus said "Seek first the Kingdom of God "and everything else will be added to you.

When you are driving and the distance is quite a longer than you would like. The eyes are alert to looking for a place to relax or get something to eat. The ears are listing to your thoughts as direction is in the seeking mode. The very ideal of a GPS mapping your objective destiny and you following a four inch square, would have been years ago unthinkable. But as time is invested so results come from desires and aspiration is the meditation of tomorrow.

What you see is what you get, so what do you want in life and what will you do with it. As for me personally; I want to kick some Lucifer butt, destroy all that he has done in people's lives and to see the joy of the Lord with lives changing from Glory to Glory. I want you to see that Jesus is the Spirit of Prophecy and that He knows my future and He believes in me. So when someone believes in you, that is theperson to spend the most time with.

For in the time invested, will be the result of time returned. For time the unfound friend will invite other friends of his to come and see the person that desired wisdom and sought knowledge while overcoming excuses, feelings, distractions while following the path of righteousness and finding favor with God and man! Enjoy life and have fun by building a strong friendship with a unfound friend called time.

Notes_____

_____

_____

Chapter 8

Faithful in the Small Things Brings Success

To whom much is given, much is required

(Luke 12:48), this statement alone causes humanity and all of Christianity to be held accountable of being good stewards of the priceless commodity called time. Managing what you have can open the door for more. Jesus said that if you can be faithful with little, you can be rewarded with much (Luke 16:10).

Procrastination is a disease of the dysfunctional mind that looks at the moment and does not count the cost of tomorrow.

*Notes*_____

_____

_____

Late fees are the trail of the procrastination, while saving step at a time. Jesus said give no place to the devil, knowwhat Jesus said opens up the understanding of the prince of accounts are the opportunity of those that pursue a vision one darkness causes us not to see the results of being rresponsible James 4:17 tells us that "it is sin for those that know to do good and do it not."

The same accountability is upon the believer in that Romans 14:23 tells us that what is not of faith is sin. Just for those that do not understand, sin is anything that separates you from the favor and presence of God. In Luke 12:42-48 tells of a man that was a stewart or manager of someone else's money and properties,

Notes_____

_____

_____

Jesus makes this statement "Who, then, is the faithful and careful servant manager whom his master will put in charge of giving all his other servants their share of food at the right time?. Then in Matthew 25 tells us of five wise and five foolish virgins or also known as brides maids. Matthew 25:23 when you have been faithful over a little; I will set you over much. These stories in comparison have to do with management and oversight. Also here is a story of a leader without patience about a debt someone else owed in Matthew 18:23-34.

In Luke 16:10-13 the statement is made about management and oversight, the subject is about trust and ability, and if ye have not been faithful in that which is another man's, who shall give you that which is your own? Then Jesus tells a story of three men and the management and oversight of money with the investment of time in Luke 22. All four of these scriptures give identity to management of time. Each one is speaking of managing your mind to manage time and the resources entrusted to you.

The reality of oversight and management has all to do with what you do with what you got. Not dreaming about what you want and have not. What can God trust you with, if you cannot manage your time, it's because you cannot manage your mind. Whether its forgiveness to others or being bigger than other people's problems.

Love covers a multitude of sins. But if are gripping and harping on other people's past of what they did or did not do, this alone can hinder your success and alter your destiny. That is why Philippians 3:13 tells us to

Notes_____

_____

has happened, but to those that recreate their past by wasting time describing the one-sided view of circumstances with contempt. To those, who live in the past, you are destroying forget those things that are behind you. Is the past worth the time invested, to dig up the dead and crucify again those that you have not forgiven. We can't change what your future and imperiling your moment. No one drives a car backward all the time, only to get to a place to turn around.

In Joshua 1:8 God speaks clearly to the servant of Moses and instructs him in what it will take to succeed in Moses place, since Moses death. The clearing of one's mind takes more than a moment it takes time. God told Joshua to meditate upon the Word of God day and night that he could lead and make choices that cause success for all.

Notes_____

Changing today, while creating tomorrow begins by managing your time and managing your mind! II Corinthians 10: 5 Casting down thoughts that disagree with what God has said about you and bring every thought into fulfillment and opportunity by speaking what God says about you.

Self-worth helps create physical wealth on this earth, for when you believe in yourself, you can weather the storm created by those that do not believe in you. Remember the unfound friend will speak in your life to confirm and affirm if you can find discipline to control you life beyond circumstances.

Notes_____

_____

_____

_____

_____

Chapter 9

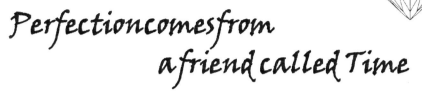

Perfectioncomesfrom a friend called Time

I heard a statement some time ago "that excellence was tolerated and perfection was required." There is nothing perfect until it stands the test of time, pressure and internal strength. Confrontation always exposes what you are made of, and at times your strength is there and at other times your weaknesses can be exposed. Time is the initiator of perfection because correction is proof that perfection has not been obtained. Perfection is only obtained with the proof that only a friend called time brings one to. Perfection is being without flaw. Even Jesus was not perfect till He overcame all temptations. He was pure, innocent, walked with integrity and every confrontation brought excellence.

Notes_____

The scripture of Hebrews 5:7-8 tell us " While he (Jesus) lived on earth, anticipating death, Jesus cried out in pain and wept in sorrow as he offered up priestly prayers to God. Because he honored God, God answered him. Though he was God's Son, he learned trusting-obedience by what he suffered, just as we do. Then, having arrived at the full stature of his maturity and having been announced by God as high priest in the order of Melchizedek, he became the source of eternal salvation to all who believingly obey him (MSG)".

It's like the deliver of my children, the time and pain of the delivery their mother went through, brought me to a lesson I learned of never holding the hand of a woman in labor,

Notes_____

_____

_____

she was stronger than Samson. The miracle of any child being born starts at conception; this took time from the beginning till the wonderful birth took place of a human being which could actually change the world.

In the book of Psalms 139:13-14 *"Oh yes, you shaped me first inside, then out; you formed me in my mother's womb. I thank you, High God—you're breathtaking! Body and soul, I am marvelously made! I worship in adoration you, what a creation! You know me inside and out, you know every bone in my body; You know exactly how I was made, bit by bit, how I was sculpted from nothing into something. Like an open book, you watched me grow from conception to birth; all the stages of my life were spread out before you, the days of my life all prepared before I'd even lived one day"* (MSG).

Notes_____

_____

Chapter 10

Knowing Destiny is Hinged upon Pursuits

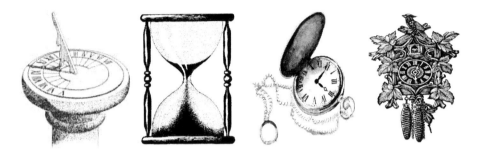

In our daily lives or in a world war, in a relationship being casual or intimate, even in business or in law, time is required to give priority for accomplishment. The main issue is timing, even the stock markets around the world; the main issue is timing. Timing is opportunity seized or missed, **timing is strategy and strategy is timing.** Remember in time of war, **if your enemy can distract you, he can attack you.** In all of life whether prodigy or developed skill, the process of learning and creating the unconscious strength of confidence requires finding your greatest support individual called time.

Destiny is opportunity and opportunity is responsibility. To acquire it you have to desire it. For what you do with today will always affect tomorrow even in the smallest way. As stated in Proverbs 29:18 "Without a vision, people perish, they are left hopeless.

Being hopeless means weak, indifferent, no drive, no discipline or self-motivation. It takes nine months for a child to be born, but it takes seconds to conceive. Without a vision a desired place of accomplisment life is void.

DESTINY IS OPPORTUNITY AND OPPORTUNITY IS RESPONSIBILITY!

Notes_____

_____

_____

_____

You may have a vision or passionate desire to accomplish something in your life. But to live a dream, you must have a dream. As stated by Martin Luther King Jr. whose famous words "I have a dream" have resounded around the world. This one statement has moved mountains, changed culture and built a future as individuals took hold of his dream and became part of its fulfillment. Even Mahatma Gandhi said "The future depends on what we do in the present." Protecting time is as much as protection of an innocent child. Time starts out right, but then distractions start taking place and then you see change all over the place that has distorted, distracted and then misplaced diligence.

Time is like an infant though it grows and changes without your oversight. Same thing as with a child, he/she will grow and change into something that is different than your dream, desire and identity of acceptance.

Being a good manager, parent and steward is being responsible in guarding as you would guard a child. Being successful has no minimal or maximum time limit. Success wants to spend as much time as possible with time being the unconscionable intimate, passionate investment to bring an outcome which has no restraint or limits.

Time management is dream responsibility, and this is a relational investment.

Desires are as an acronym for unconscionable pursuits. These desires and pursuits many times have to be guarded, guided, and grounded in foundational truths. The integrity of the heart is the place to start. Starting out right does not guarantee ending with the same motive as you started with. As stated by King David in Proverbs 4:23 for his son Solomon to guard his heart. Telling Solomon to protect the integrity of his own heart, for life is shaped and created and destiny is hinged upon how one pursues even daily affairs.

The truth is, what you compromise to get, you ultimately lose.

As Paul the Apostle wrote in First Timothy 6:10 that the Love of Money is the root of all evil. Not money, but the love of it; the craving, passionate desire of fulfillment that money can create. Ecclesiastes 10:19 tells us that "Money answers all things". This can be so true in many issues. But, when money takes the place of trust, integrity or even the most powerful word of respect. Relationships are destroyed and built.

Notes_____

_____

_____

around money. The old saying is "a rich man can buy friends, but a poor man can borrow them." Knowing Destiny can attribute the importance of Time which is the issue of what is invested always brings about a return.

As stated in Galatians 6:8 "Those that makes provision for the indulgence of fleshly appetites and passions; shall experience the rewards of corruption." The keyword here is balance, believe me balance just like time can be hard to find. Management is as much an investment in your relationship with Time as a work schedule could be overwhelming.

Without the word called balance, a marriage can be destroyed, health can be depleted, and money can disappear. It's like the old statement "When your output is more than your input, your output is your downfall." It's like gaining a degree from a university; it requires research, study and then application. Destiny is hinged upon Pursuits; a diploma in undergraduate or a Masters in a certain category all require the sacrifice of Time in areas and invested in others.

Time that is divided can be a landslide as issues accumulate and the weighand responsibility increase. Remember my professor at University of Phoenix t taught me a statement I will never forget. "You do what you can do, delegate what you can delegate, delay what you can delay and then delete the rest."

Destiny many times comes with the purpose of creation as listed in Psalms 139:13- 18 or in Jeremiah 1:5. Destiny is opportunity, but destiny is hinged on pursuit. Even if a child is born a prodigy in music, still it takes pursuit of sitting at the keyboard of a piano or the strings of a violin. For gifts to come forth one learns the details of precision and excellence to play such music as Mozart or Beethoven. Knowing Destiny is hinged upon pursuits allows you to keep focus on your responsibility and patience to accomplish your desires.

The element of surprise will be when destiny is before your eyes and you realize that your dream has come true. Your assignment from God has completely manifested and the next level is the greater calling of accomplishment by means of greater responsibility. Remember, responsibility is your response to your ability, not just opportunity. Knowing Destiny is Hinged upon Pursuits helps keep focus.

*Notes*_____

_____

_____

_____

_____

Some things in life only happen when commitment of pursuits happens. Standing still many times never makes sense when it seems you can do it now. But when the word of the Lord to you is in trusting Him; He will take care of you. This at times seems to not come in line with the word called responsibility. Time the unfound friend does not make sense when God has chosen to require you to hold His hand and let Him take command.

It's when the situation seems to fall apart as you watch and cry from your heart, God what can I do to fix it other than just trust you. Spend Time with God's word and presence. Learn He controls the speed of light; He can give you insight on how to change everything. When trust is destroyed, it destroys the relationship.

Notes_____

_____

Our destiny is in God's hands as much as ours. The deep heart felt trust is not based on results in the moment as much as the trust in the promise will be fulfilled. Trust is a choice, not a feeling, feelings are deceptive. Feelings are like vertigo in an airplane, you're not sure if you are upside down or even headed flying up or down. Principle is a standard of truth andeven hidden from the eyes of people; truth will surface and expose the lies.

You much take responsibility for how you allow yourself to think, talk and even meditate. Trusting God and continue to believe in your destiny is not circumstantial, but providential. The cry of your spirit, the deepness of your heart and soul, cries for fulfillment, accomplishment.

Notes_____

_____

From the descriptive words of Mahatma Gandhi speak very clear in this statement, "Your beliefs become your thoughts. Your thoughts become your words. Your words become your actions. Your actions become your habits. Your habits become your values. Your values become your destiny. What you do with Time is what you do with tomorrow.

When you cannot find the Unfound Friend called Time, neither do you find tomorrow in your today. If security, while not focusing on opportunity. Destiny is not just a promise but an assignment, a responsibility of clarity that affects other people's destiny. You as an individual play a major role in other people's lives, including their future and opportunities.

Notes_____ _____

_____

Destiny is hinged on your pursuit, as the Apostle Paul said, "fight the good fight of faith" and faith is based on trust not feelings. In the book of Romans chapter eleven verse twenty nine the prophet spoke a strong word of responsibility. "For the gifts and the calling of God are irrevocable (World English Bible)".

Many do not realize that their work profession is their calling and their specialty is their giftings from God. Whether it is Doctor, Lawyer, Pastor, Teacher, Musician, Entertainer, Songwriter or Singer. Destiny is always connecting destinies to destiny to bring about the long term plan of God in people's lives.

My grandmother told me a story of a when she was a little girl. She was with her little sister and brother walking home from school. As the evening was setting, the walk from school had a long distance and they heard the wolves howling from the distance. They began to call on the name of Jesus as they hurried their pace to get home. They saw the wolves from a distance so they crawled inside this hollow tree that crossed the creek. Usually they walked over the big fallen tree that crossed the creek. They knew the wolves could outrun them, so they stayed inside of the tree praying. Wolves had blocked both ends of the hollow tree and as they prayed for the help of Jesus, then they heard their Dad yell,

"I'm coming". The wolves left as they heard the gun shots blast and the yelling of family coming to the aid of three children. No one knew a family of Gospel singers and musicians would come to be invited on the Roy Rogers Show. No matter how it looks at times, God will put people in your life to assist your Unfound Friend to take hold of destiny with you. The creative hand of God creates opportunity of unity, by not letting anything overwhelm you as Destiny calls your name. Remember Destiny is about life's assignment for fulfillment. Your life, your destiny has friends and family that God puts to help time be your friend no matter what the problem might be.

Destiny could be all about, words or worlds by choice. It's all about the power of agreement. When you have a dream unfulfilled, do you yield to despair or fight for what desired Destiny in you does declare. We can recreate our past or create our future in what we pursue, apply to do, follow through or even the people we listen too. In Romans 11:29 says, "For the gifts and calling of God are without exchange or debate. This in simple words means God requires results, while excuses are non-acceptable. All of your Destiny Hinges upon your pursuit. Your attitude has authority, influence and resolve; this is setting inmotion the results of you are known by the company you keep. When you have a God given gift, assignment and destiny; you will always have the responsibility of protecting your future. This is by the investments of your moments also known as Time the Unfound Friend, because each moment shapes one's future.

For what you feed grows and what you starve dies. Do not destroy your future by letting others control the time required to accomplish your dream. It takes time to learn a foreign language, to develop the brush strokes which define the artist you are. The rhythm, the beat the style of music that moves your feet. Never stand still when Destiny is crying out to be fulfilled. Look for, seek out and find Time the Unfound Friend to succeed, to accomplish and fulfill your assignment on the earth.

Then Jesus can say, "Well done thou good and faithful servant." Dr. Mark D. White © 2015

BLOOD OF JESUS CHRIST PRAYER

I CLAIM (RECEIVE WITH THANKSGIVING) THE POWER OF THE BLOOD OF JESUS AND HIS COMPLETED WORK ON THE CROSS OF CALVARY OVER MY LIFE TODAY. I BRING THE POWER OF CHRIST'S REDEMPTION WITH ALL OF ITS JUSTIFYING, RECONCILING, PROPITIATING, REGENERATING, HEALING, DELIVERING, REDEEMING, CLEANSING, SANCTIFYING, PROTECTING, AND CONSECRATING POWER OVER THE DOORPOSTS AND LINTELS OF MY LIFE. I APPLY THE BLOOD AND THE CROSS OVER MY OWN LIFE AND THAT OF MY BLOODLINE FAMILY MEMBERS AS WELL AS MY SPOUSE AND THEIR BLOODLINE FAMILY MEMBERS. I CLAIM THE BLOOD'S POWER OVER MY SPIRIT, MY SOUL, AND MY BODY, OVER MY MIND, MY WILL AND MY EMOTIONS. OVER MY CONSCIOUS, SUBCONSCIOUS, AND UNCONSIOUS MIND.
I RECEIVE THE POWER OF CHRIST'S REDEMPTION OVER MY PAST, MY PRESENT, AND MY FUTURE.

I CLAIM THE FINISHED WORK OF THE CROSS AND THE BLOOD OF CHRIST OVER EVERY AREA OF LIFE WHERE FATHER INTENDS BLESSING FOR ME. OVER MY HEALTH, FINANCES, HOME, BUSINESS, MINISTRY, TRAVEL, TOOLS OF SERVICE INCLUDING VEHICLES, COMPUTERS AND ALL ELECTRONIC EQUIPMENT AND EVERYTHING THAT IS GIVEN TO ME TO SERVE AND BLESS ME AND WHERE THE ENEMY LIKES TO AFFLICT ME. I SURRENDER MY ENTIRE LIFE, MY SPIRIT, SOUL, AND BODY, MY MIND, WILL AND EMOTIONS TO YOU TODAY, HOLY SPIRIT, ASKING YOU TO DO FOR AND THROUGH ME WHAT I CANNOT DO FOR MYSELF AND THAT YOU WILL LEAD, GUIDE, AND DIRECT, CORRECT AND PROTECT ME IN THE PATHS OF YOUR CHOICE FOR MY LIFE.

AMEN

References:

Gandhi,
Mahatma: http://www.quotationspage.com/search.php3?
Search=&Author=Mahatma
+Gandhi&C=coles&C=lindsly&C=poorc&C=net&C=devils
&C=contrib&page=3

King, Martin Luther: http://www.mlkonline.net/quotes.html

World English Bible: http://biblehub.com/romans/11-29.htm

New International Version (NIV)
Holy Bible, New International Version®, NIV® Copyright © 1973, 1978, 1984, 2011 by Biblica, Inc.® Used by permission. All rights reserved worldwide.

J.R.R. Tolkien, The Fellowship of the
Ring: http://www.goodreads.com/quotes/12357-i-wish-
it-need-not-have-happened-in-my-time

Quarks; http://www.livescience.com/37206-atom-
definition.html;
http://physics.stackexchange.com/questions/31465/if-quarks-
didnt-have-mass-could-protons-and-neutrons-exist

Tiny 24-Hour Clock in Every Living
Thing; http://www.foxnews.com/scitech/2011/01/28/meet-
tiny-hour-clock-blood-cells/

Biography of Dr. Mark D. White
Expressing the Fathers Heart

Mark D. White was raised an Assembly of God pastor's son and started preaching at the age of 15. In 1978 he graduated from Kenneth E. Hagin's Rhema Bible Training Center in Tulsa, Oklahoma. Since then he has been an associate pastor of two churches, and has pastored three. Mark also holds a Doctorate from Saint Thomas University and a BS/BM from University of Phoenix. Mark is on the leadership team of Global Fire Ministries in Murfreesboro, Tn. with Jeff Jansen as team leader.

Mark travels extensively throughout the United States and travels International ministering the Word of God by precept and example. Having over 43 years active experience in ministry, gives place to the workings of the Holy Spirit in the lives of the believers and unbelievers.

Mark's insight and practical understanding in the spirit makes room for him to operate in the Prophets' office with a pastor's heart. There is a strong tangible anointing upon him, which gives place to the open move of the Holy Spirit in edifying and comforting the local church. Mark has a reputation for balanced teaching and preaching with compassion for the heart of the people. Homes are restored, blind eyes are opened, deaf ears are healed, cancers disappears, cataracts removed, and broken hearts are mended. The Word of God is preached with signs following. Miracles and Healings happen in every service. It is Marks desire to serve the purpose of each and every local church and ministry. Mark is the author of two books that expresses the Heart of God. **Your Identity: The Thumbprint of God and Time the Unfound Friend.** www.markwhite.tv Email address - zdkadar@gmail.com

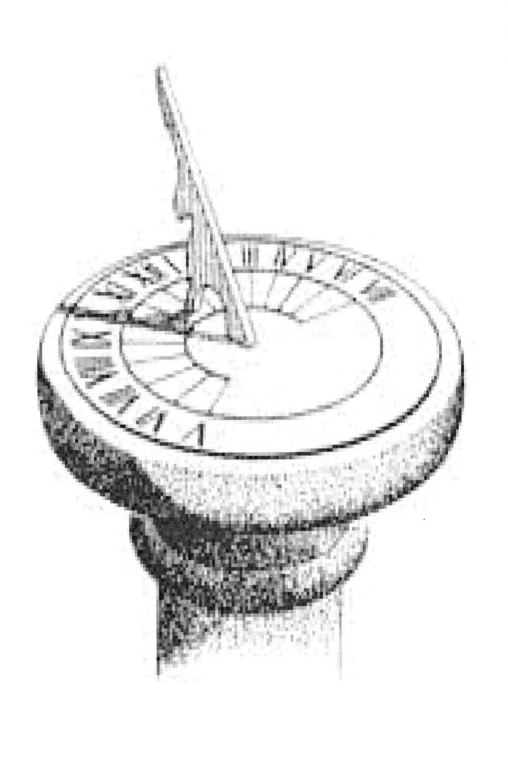